HOPE|**EXPLORED**

WHAT'S THE BEST FUTURE YOU
COULD EVER IMAGINE?

LEADER'S HANDBOOK

Hope Explored Leader's Handbook
Copyright © 2022 Christianity Explored Ministries
www.ceministries.org

Published by:
The Good Book Company Ltd

thegoodbook.com | thegoodbook.co.uk
thegoodbook.com.au | thegoodbook.co.nz | thegoodbook.co.in

CHRISTIANITY
EXPLORED
MINISTRIES

ISBN: 9781784986810 | Printed in Turkey

Design by André Parker

WELCOME TO
HOPE|EXPLORED

There are few emotions more powerful than hope. It's a spark inside you that brings a smile to your lips, a light that shows on your face, a feeling that lifts your head and pulls you forward. Hope is what keeps us alive.

These days hope often feels hard to come by. But real hope is what the Christian faith claims to offer: a joyful expectation for the future, based on true events in the past, which changes everything about my present.

Over three sessions, *Hope Explored* shows guests how the gospel infuses life with the hope, peace and purpose we all long for. We'll see how Jesus was himself the fulfilment of a promise of hope made to God's Old Testament people centuries before; and how his life, death and resurrection are the guarantee of an even greater fulfilment to come.

"May the God of hope fill you with all joy and peace as you trust in him, so that you may overflow with hope by the power of the Holy Spirit" (Romans 15:13).

The Hope Explored Team

CONTENTS

SECTION 1
HOW TO RUN
HOPE EXPLORED

REGISTER YOUR COURSE AT
WWW.HOPE.EXPLO.RED

Visit the *Hope Explored* website to register your course and gain access to additional materials:

- **Digital picture prompts** for the discussion activity

- Outlines and **transcripts** of the teaching films

- A **sample presentation** for use when running *Hope Explored* online

- Guidance for **setting up your course**, including setting up a venue, inviting guests, and choosing and training leaders

- **Promotional materials** including trailers, logos and posters

GETTING STARTED

Hope Explored is a three-session series about the person and work of Jesus, and the hope that can be found in him. It is intended to be an introduction to the gospel for those who would not consider themselves to be followers of Jesus.

Through the prophet Isaiah, God promised to send a Saviour who would be called "Wonderful Counsellor, Mighty God, Everlasting Father, Prince of Peace" (Isaiah 9:6). Through the work of Jesus that promise was fulfilled. *Hope Explored* shows how the events of Jesus' time on earth in the past can change our future and transform our present.

STRUCTURE OF THE COURSE

Each session explores an aspect of Jesus' work: his life, his death and his resurrection. Each session also explores one of the great longings we have in life: for hope, for peace and for purpose. Through teaching and studies from Luke's Gospel, Jesus is seen to be the fulfilment of God's promise through Isaiah, and the fulfilment of our greatest needs.

By exploring Jesus' life in Session 1, we see that Jesus is the Mighty God, who fulfils our longing for hope. By exploring Jesus' death in Session 2, we see that Jesus is the Prince of Peace, who makes it possible for us to have peace with God and one another. By exploring Jesus' resurrection in Session 3, we see that Jesus is the Everlasting Father, whose defeat of death gives life the purpose we're looking for. And having explored these things, we are left with a question: will you have Jesus as your Wonderful Counsellor?

The chart below shows how the course is structured and how the themes fit together.

	SESSION 1	SESSION 2	SESSION 3
Film Part 1	Hope	Peace	Purpose
Discussion activity	Where do you think the world is going?	How do you think we can find peace?	Where do you look for a sense of purpose?
Film Part 2	Luke 8:22-25, 40-56	Luke 23:32, 39-46	Luke 24:1-11, 36-44
Explore	Luke 1:1-4; 8:40-42, 49-56	Luke 23:32-47	Luke 24:1-6, 9-12, 36-44
	Jesus is the Mighty God, with the power to meet our deepest needs.	Jesus is the Prince of Peace, who tears down the barrier between us and God.	Jesus is the Everlasting Father, whose defeat of death gives life the meaning we long for.

Will you have Jesus as your Wonderful Counsellor?

KEY THEMES

As you use *Hope Explored*, look out for the following themes, which run through the material:

- **Definition of hope:** Hope is a joyful expectation for the future, based on true events in the past, which changes everything about my present.

- **Fulfilment of prophecy:** The Christian faith is based on evidence – the promises of God for the future made in the Old Testament, which were fulfilled in history in the person and work of Jesus. This in turn gives us a confident hope that God will keep his promise to bring about a new creation for his people in the future.

- **Turning points:** The events of Jesus' life, death and resurrection are the turning points of history; they can be turning points in our lives too.

STRUCTURE OF A SESSION

How and when you meet will depend on your situation. Many courses run on a midweek evening for three weeks; you may meet at a church, at home, in a coffee shop or online.

Advice and additional resources for running a course are available to download from the *Hope Explored* website at **www.hope.explo.red**.

Below is a recommended structure for a session. A key part of *Hope Explored* is building relationships with guests. You may want to consider serving a meal before the session or offering hot drinks and cake. At the end of the session, encourage guests to stay and chat further if they would like to do so.

- **Film Part 1** | 10 minutes
- **Discussion activity** | 15 minutes
- **Film Part 2** | 20 minutes
- **Explore** | 30 minutes

The **Film Part 1** introduces the theme of the session.

The **Discussion activity** gives guests the opportunity to share their views on the theme of the session. Picture prompts are provided to spark discussion. These are included in the Handbook, but the activity will work better for groups if everyone is looking at a larger set of pictures together. These can be purchased from The Good Book Company or downloaded from **www.hope. explo.red** to print out or display on a screen.

The **Film Part 2** contains teaching from Luke's Gospel. It picks up on the theme of the session and shows how it finds its fulfilment in the person and work of Jesus. Alternatively you may prefer to give the Bible teaching live, in person. The transcripts of both parts of the films are included at the back of this Leader's Handbook for your use, and can also be downloaded from the *Hope Explored* website.

The **Explore** section gives guests the opportunity to read and discuss a Bible passage for themselves. The questions reinforce and explore in more depth the material covered in the teaching film. This Leader's Handbook contains notes with additional guidance for leaders.

REQUIRED MATERIALS

To use *Hope Explored* most effectively, you will need the following materials:

• A copy of **Luke's Gospel** or a **Bible** for each leader and guest. The Bible version used in the *Hope Explored* materials and teaching films is the New International Version (NIV 2011).

• A copy of the **Handbook** for each guest and a copy of the **Leader's Handbook** for each leader.

• Pens, to allow guests to make notes or jot down questions.

• A copy of the **picture prompts** for the **discussion activity** for each small group. (Optional but recommended – see above.)

REGISTER YOUR COURSE

Visit **www.hope.explo.red** to register your course. This gives you access to a range of additional resources, which can be downloaded and used or adapted for your context:

- **Picture prompts** for the discussion activity

- Outlines and **transcripts** of the teaching films

- Sample **presentation** for use when running *Hope Explored* online

- Guidance for **setting up your course**, including setting up a venue, inviting guests, and choosing and training leaders

- **Promotional materials** including trailers, logos, and posters

The **www.hope.explo.red** website also contains information about the *Christianity Explored* and *Life Explored* series. *Hope Explored* is an introduction to the person and work of Jesus, but after three sessions many guests will be left wanting more. Consider following this series with *Christianity Explored* or *Life Explored* to help your guests to continue exploring the Christian faith.

BEFORE THE COURSE

Before the course starts, there are a number of things you should do.

GET TO KNOW LUKE'S GOSPEL, THE HANDBOOK AND THE FILMS

Read through the Bible passages, and through the whole of Luke's Gospel to set them in context. Familiarize yourself with the Handbook that your group will be using and the guidance on the answers to questions in the study-guide section of this Leader's Handbook (page 27).

As you prepare, you might find it helpful to make notes in your copy of the group members' Handbook. Some people prefer to use an annotated Handbook to lead their group instead of referring back to this Leader's Handbook. Either way, you will feel much more confident to lead your group once you've prepared for the Bible studies and discussions.

As your group members journey through *Hope Explored*, you will need to be prepared to answer questions that arise from the teaching films and from the Bible text. There is a section on page 65 that will help you prepare for these questions in advance. If, during the session, you don't know the answer to someone's question, just acknowledge the fact and ask if you can find the answer in time for the next session.

If you are using the *Hope Explored* films, watch each episode through several times. This will help you to become more familiar with the material and also enable you to refer back to it during discussion: "Do you remember what was said in the film?"

PREPARE YOUR PERSONAL STORY

"Always be prepared to give an answer to everyone who asks you to give the reason for the hope that you have. But do this with gentleness and respect..."

(1 Peter 3:15)

A personal story or testimony is an account of God's work in your life. Everybody who has been born again and who is becoming like Christ has a unique, interesting and powerful story, regardless of whether or not it appears spectacular.

At some point during the course, you may feel it appropriate to share your story with the group. Often someone will ask you directly how you became a Christian, and you will need to have an answer ready.

You may find the guidelines below helpful as you prepare your story:

- Keep it honest, personal and interesting.

Tip: Your first sentence should make people sit up and listen. Anything too dull-sounding – for example, "Well, I don't have a very interesting story" – may make people switch off immediately.

- Keep it short.

Tip: Any more than three minutes may stretch people's patience. They can always ask you questions if they want to know more.

- Keep pointing to Christ, not yourself.

Tip: Your story is a great opportunity to communicate the gospel. Always include what it is that you believe, as well as how you came to believe it. As a general guide, try to explain why you think Jesus is God, how his death affects you personally, and what changes God has made in your life.

- *Prepare your personal story. (List the main points below.) You might find it useful to share your story with other leaders and get their feedback.*

_____

_____

PREPARE FOR DIFFICULT QUESTIONS

As you look at the Bible with guests and discuss the claims of Christianity, it is likely to draw out a number of questions that will need careful handling. The appendices, starting on page 63, will help you deal with some of the most common questions that people may ask.

PRAY

- that those invited will attend the course.
- that God would enable you to prepare well.
- for the logistics of organizing the course.
- for good relationships with your co-leaders and group members.
- that God would equip you to lead faithfully.
- that the Holy Spirit would open the blind eyes of those who attend.

GOD'S ROLE IN EVANGELISM
AND OURS

We need to distinguish between God's role in evangelism and our role. It's going to be incredibly frustrating if we try to fulfil God's role – because only the Creator of the universe is able to do that.

Read 2 Corinthians 4:1-6

Answer the following questions from the verses you've just read:

What is God's role in evangelism?

Why can't people see the truth of the gospel?

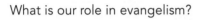

What is our role in evangelism?

How should we carry out our role in evangelism?

GOD'S ROLE IN EVANGELISM

What is God's role in evangelism? God makes "his light shine in our hearts to give us the light of the knowledge of God's glory displayed in the face of Christ" (2 Corinthians 4:6).

In other words, God enables us to recognize that Jesus is God. God makes it possible – by his Holy Spirit – for a person to see who Jesus is. When Paul is on the Damascus road, he asks, "Who are you, Lord?" and is told, "I am Jesus" (Acts 9:5). That is the moment of his conversion – when he recognizes for the first time who Jesus actually is.

The beginning of 2 Corinthians 4:6 reminds us that God said, "Let light shine out of darkness". That is a reference to the miracle of creation in Genesis 1:3. This same God, who brought light into the world at creation, now shines light into the hearts of human beings, enabling them to see that Jesus is God. In other words, for people to recognize that Jesus is God, God must perform a miracle.

People do not become Christians just because we share the gospel with them. God must shine his light in people's hearts so that they recognize and respond to the truth of the gospel.

And we know from 2 Corinthians 4:4 that people can't see the truth of the gospel because "the god of this age has blinded the minds of unbelievers".

Here, Paul reminds us that we are in the midst of a supernatural battlefield. The reason so many reject the gospel is that the devil is at work, preventing people from recognizing who Jesus is.

The devil blinds people by making them chase after the things of this world, which are passing away and which cannot save them. Their concerns are confined to the here-and-now: their popularity, their family, their relationships, their material possessions. They are blind to anything beyond that.

As a result, they can only see Jesus in the here-and-now, perhaps only as a great moral teacher; his eternal significance is completely obscured. And, according to verse 4, Satan is determined to prevent people from seeing "the light of the gospel that displays the glory of Christ, who is the image of God". Satan does not want people to recognize who Jesus is.

OUR ROLE IN EVANGELISM

What then is our role in evangelism? "We preach ... Jesus Christ as Lord" (2 Corinthians 4:5).

The word "preach" can evoke negative images, but it derives from a word simply meaning "herald": someone who relates important announcements from the king to his kingdom. Our role is to tell people the gospel and leave the Spirit of God to convict them of its truth.

These verses also reveal the attitude we should adopt as we preach. We are to be like "servants for Jesus' sake" (2 Corinthians 4:5). The word translated "servants" literally means "slaves" in Greek. Paul was determined to present Christ to others without any hint of self-promotion.

We must remember that the only difference between ourselves and an unbeliever is that God, in his mercy, has opened our blind eyes and illuminated our hearts by his Holy Spirit. We should be forever grateful and so seek to promote Christ, not ourselves.

We must keep preaching Christ as Lord and, remembering that only a miracle from God can open blind eyes, we must keep praying that God will shine his light in the hearts of unbelievers.

2 Corinthians 4:1-6 also helps us to carry out our role in the right way: "We do not use deception, nor do we distort the word of God ... By setting forth the truth plainly we commend ourselves to everyone's conscience in the sight of God ... For what we preach is not ourselves, but Jesus Christ as Lord."

When we tell people about Christ, we should demonstrate the following qualities:

Integrity – "We do not use deception." We are straight with people; we are genuine and sincere, and we never use any kind of emotional manipulation.

Fidelity – We do not "distort the word of God". We have to tell people the tough bits. If, for example, we don't tell people about sin, about hell, and about the necessity of repentance, then we are distorting God's word. Preaching these hard truths means trusting in the work of the Holy Spirit to draw people to Christ, however "difficult" the message.

Humility – "What we preach is not ourselves, but Jesus Christ as Lord." We must draw people to Jesus, not to ourselves. We must remember that some people are very impressionable, and that we want them to make a decision to follow Christ because they are convinced by the truth and are being led by the Holy Spirit, rather than being manipulated by their admiration of the course leader.

As we use *Hope Explored* to preach the gospel, we must remember that it is up to God whether somebody becomes a Christian or not. Only he can open blind eyes, so we must trust him for the results.

HELPING SOMEONE WHO WANTS TO FOLLOW CHRIST

When someone shares with you their desire to follow Christ for the first time, it's surely one of the most joyous privileges of the Christian life.

But, like Jesus, we need to be clear – from the outset – about what prospective believers are getting themselves into. In Luke 14, Jesus says, "Whoever does not carry their cross and follow me cannot be my disciple. Suppose one of you wants to build a tower. Won't you first sit down and estimate the cost to see if you have enough money to complete it? For if you lay the foundation and are not able to finish it, everyone who sees it will ridicule you, saying, 'This person began to build and wasn't able to finish'" (Luke 14:27-30).

Grace may be free, but it is not cheap. It cost Jesus his life. And Jesus calls us to give up our lives too, if we want to follow him. The invitation may be extended to all, but only those who obey Jesus' call – to carry their cross – can receive it.

So when we find ourselves in the privileged position of helping someone who wants to follow Christ, we must be clear about what following him will mean for them.

And according to Jesus, it means we must "repent and believe" (Mark 1:15). This won't be easy in a world which rejects Jesus and those who want to follow him.

- Explain that "**repent**" means we turn around from the direction we're currently heading in and turn back to God. We start living life to please him, rather than continuing to rebel against him.

- Explain that "**believe**" means we believe that Jesus is who he says he is and that he died for our sin on the cross – and we're putting our trust in him as a result.

So to repent and believe is something that we do decisively at a moment in time, but it is not just a moment to look back on; it is a new, ongoing way of life. Help your guest to see what repentance and belief will look like in their daily lives:

- **A new attitude to God.** A follower of Jesus is deeply thankful to God, and longs to know him better and love him more. This longing is nurtured by reading the Bible, praying and spending time with his people.

  Encourage your guest by offering to read the Bible one to one with them, and suggesting some daily Bible-reading notes. A follow-up course like *Discipleship Explored* is also a great way for a new believer to get started.

  Encourage them to pray to God about what they've discovered on *Hope Explored*, thanking him for Jesus and what he means to them. Assure them that they can speak freely in their own words, because God sees our hearts and understands our deepest longings, even if our words are hesitant and uncertain.

- **A new attitude to God's people.** A follower of Jesus longs to love and serve their Christian brothers and sisters – and, in turn, be loved and served by them.

  This shows itself when a new believer commits themselves to a local church – a particular body of believers they can love. As Jesus said, "Love one another. As I have loved you, so you must love one another. By this everyone will know that you are my disciples, if you love one another" (John 13:34-35).

  Jesus also commanded his followers to be baptized (Matthew 28:18-20) as a way of publicly identifying with Christ and his people. Encourage your guest to speak to their pastor or minister about being baptized.

  Offer to meet your guest at church on Sunday and help them to establish a pattern of attending each week. Encourage them to join a small group and to use whatever skills they have in serving their brothers and sisters in Christ.

- **A new attitude to ourselves.** A follower of Jesus longs to please him by rejecting sin and living for Jesus instead.

There will be areas of our lives which we know – or will come to see – are not pleasing to Jesus. To repent and believe means that we willingly turn away from those ways of living and try to live life in the way God intends. This is the life Jesus described as life "to the full" (John 10:10).

- **A new attitude to others.** A follower of Jesus seeks to love others.

We're called to reflect Christ by relating to others with love, looking for ways to treat them as we would treat ourselves: "So in everything, do to others what you would have them do to you" (Matthew 7:12). And one aspect of that love for others will be our desire to tell them the good news about what Jesus has done.

SECTION 2
HOPE|EXPLORED SESSIONS

INTRODUCTION

This section contains each of the three sessions you'll be exploring with your guest(s). It includes all the material in their Handbook, plus additional notes and answers intended for leaders.

- Don't worry if you don't have time to go through all of the questions – the most important thing is to listen to the guests and answer their questions.

- Try to avoid using jargon, which might alienate group members. Bear in mind that words and phrases familiar to Christians may seem strange to those outside Christian circles.

- If anyone misses a session, bring them up to speed before you start. The film summaries will help you do this.

- Some guests may feel that the Bible isn't reliable as a source of history. That's a great question to raise, but it can take a while to answer well. There is some time to discuss it in the Explore section in Session 1. You can also follow up one to one at the end of the session or recommend a book such as *Can I Really Trust the Bible?* by Barry Cooper or *Can We Trust the Gospels?* by Peter J. Williams.

Key

▷ Watch a film

≡ Discuss a question

📖 Explore a Bible passage

SESSION 1
HOPE

- *If you're using these sessions in a group context, welcome the guests to Hope Explored and introduce yourself. Make sure everyone has been introduced to each other. Try to remember names ready for next week.*

- *Give a brief introduction. If you have more than one discussion group, this is best given by the course leader or speaker to everyone together. (The wording below is intended only as a general guide.)*

As we begin, I want to reassure you that:

- you won't be asked to read aloud, pray, sing or do anything that makes you feel uncomfortable.

- we aren't going to take your phone number and pester you. If you decide not to come back, we are still delighted you made time to come today.

- you can ask any question you want, or alternatively feel free just to sit and listen.

Over the next three sessions, we're going to be thinking about some of the big questions of life: How can we find hope in a world of frequent disappointment? Is there any hope of us living at peace with ourselves and with one another? Where can we find a sense of purpose that will infuse our lives with genuine meaning?

We also want to spend time addressing whatever questions are important to you. As well as having times of discussion in groups, we will be available to chat at the end of the session.

Please feel free to make notes and list questions you may have as you watch the films. There is space for notes in your Handbook.

Give each guest a Luke's Gospel or Bible and a Handbook.

Ask the group to turn to Session 1 on page 7 of the Handbook.

- *Explain how the evening will run.*

    Watch Part 1: We watch an introduction to this session's theme.
    Discussion: We have an opportunity to discuss our own views and experiences in relation to the theme.
    Watch Part 2: We watch a film teaching something from the Bible.
    Explore: We read that part of the Bible and discuss it together.

(▷) **WATCH: Hope Part 1 (approx 6 mins)**

- Hope is a wonderful thing – but few things are more crushing than when our hopes are disappointed.

- A hope worth having needs to…
    - be true.
    - deliver what it promises.
    - be for something that will last.

- The Christian faith is all about hope: a joyful expectation for the future, based on true events in the past, which changes everything about my present.

⊜ DISCUSS

---

*This activity makes use of four picture prompts, each representing
a view of where the world is going. The pictures are provided in the
Handbook, but to make this activity more dynamic, it's recommended
that you print out or purchase a larger set of pictures (see page 12), so
that they can be spread in front of you and passed between you as you
discuss them together.*

*Ask the question below, and then briefly explain the pictures and
what they represent, but don't worry about nailing down specific
definitions. Encourage guests to choose the one which resonates most
with them. This is an opportunity to listen to guests as they share their
understanding of hope, and the things they place their hope in.*

**How much hope we have will depend on where we've been, where we are,
and where we think we're going. Some of us may be searching for hope;
others of us may be more sceptical. What about you? Where do you think
the world is going?**

Things are getting worse: The course of history leaves us hopeless. Human
beings are on course to destroy the planet. Climate change will destroy us if
war and global pandemics don't. Our lives used to be better than they are
now, and it looks as if they won't recover.

Things are getting better: The course of history leaves us hopeful. Human
beings are making progress in politics, technology and healthcare. The world
faces big problems, but we are innovating good solutions. Our lives used to
be worse than they are now, and it looks as if they will keep improving.

Things go round in a circle of life: History is going round in circles. Nations
rise and fall. The seasons come and go. We've seen it all before, and we'll see
it all again.

Things are in chaos: History is governed by random events. Human beings are each a collection of atoms, ruled by chemical and electrical impulses. Nature is unpredictable and uncontrollable. We don't know where we've come from, and we can't know where we're going.

It may be that members of your group find that a combination of these resonate, or they have their own ideas. To stimulate discussion, you could ask some follow-up questions: How would you – or your parents – have answered when you were growing up? What significant life events have changed your attitude towards hope? How would you answer differently if you were asked about the world in general, and then about your life in particular?

Things are getting worse

Things are getting better

Things go round in a circle of life

Things are in chaos

(▷) **WATCH: Hope Part 2 (approx 16 mins)**

(Page 9 in the group members' Handbook.) Encourage people to make notes or write down questions as they watch the teaching film.

- Life is full of many good things. But the Bible is realistic about the darkness we experience too.

- Isaiah 9 speaks to "people walking in darkness". It was a message from God, promising his people a "Wonderful Counsellor, Mighty God, Everlasting Father, Prince of Peace", who would bring light to the darkness (Isaiah 9:6).

- Most of us hope that there's a God out there. The Bible says that there *is*, and that he's come to earth in the person of Jesus. Jesus is the person Isaiah spoke of.

- Jesus calmed a storm on Lake Galilee.

- Jesus raised a dead girl.

- There's only one category big enough for him: Mighty God.

- Jesus proves there is a Mighty God who cares for his world and wants to help people.

- Jesus' miracles point to the end of the story: one day he will bring in full a new world without uncertainty, sickness or grief.

- This is the Christian hope: a joyful expectation for the future, based on true events in the past, that changes everything about the present.

² The people walking in darkness
have seen a great light;
on those living in the land of deep darkness
a light has dawned ...
⁶ For to us a child is born,
to us a son is given,
and the government will be on his shoulders.
And he will be called
Wonderful Counsellor, Mighty God,
Everlasting Father, Prince of Peace.

Isaiah 9:2, 6

📖 EXPLORE

1. What most surprised or intrigued you about the Christian view of hope that we've just heard described?

This question aims to give guests an opportunity to respond to what they've just heard, if they'd like to. It's fine to keep this conversation short if guests don't have much that they want to share.

Christian hope claims to be "a joyful expectation for the future based on true events in the past". The question is: how do we know those events are true? In the film, we heard about one day in Jesus' life, as told by a man named Luke in his "Gospel". So, can we trust Luke's account?

Right at the beginning of his book, Luke describes how he went about compiling his Gospel.

Help group members to find Luke 1:1-4 in their copy of Luke's Gospel or Bible. You may want to take this opportunity to explain how Bible chapter and verse references work.

Read Luke 1:1-4

("Luke 1:1-4" refers to Luke, chapter 1, verses 1-4.)

2. According to Luke, why did he write his Gospel? (See Luke 1:4.)

Luke wanted his readers to have "certainty of the things you have been

---

Fulfilled | Brought about; completed.
Eye witnesses | Those who saw first-hand what Jesus said and did.
The word | God's message about Jesus.

Theophilus | A Greek name meaning "friend of God". This was the first, though not the only reader of Luke's book.

---

taught". Theophilus had clearly already heard Christian teaching (just like the people in your group will over the course of these *Hope Explored* sessions). But he needed to be able to know its "certainty" – that the things he'd heard about Jesus really happened and were really true. You could follow up by asking, "Why is it important to have certainty about the teaching about Jesus, do you think?" If we don't have that certainty, then we can't enjoy solid hope. Our view of the future will be dogged by doubt or despair. But if we are confident that Jesus is who he said he is, we can be certain that his wonderful promises about the future will come true.

3. How did Luke research the events he wrote about? (See Luke 1:2-3.)

He acted like a modern-day journalist or historian.

- He spoke with eye witnesses (v 2) and "servants of the word" (those who were sharing the news that "things ... have been fulfilled").

- He "carefully investigated everything" (v 3). It seems that Luke did not just believe everything he'd been told, but checked, cross-referenced, followed-up etc. Luke is not presenting us with a fairytale or embellished legend. He's telling us what really took place.

- He aimed to "write an orderly account" (v 3). He'd clearly thought about what to include, in what order, etc.

4. How does Luke's method help us to have confidence in what he wrote about Jesus?

As the Part 1 film emphasised, Christianity is not about a feeling in my tummy or a blind faith in defiance of the data. It starts with information, which we are called to put our trust in. These true events in the past are the basis of Christian hope.

You might also like to point out that Luke wrote about "the things that have been fulfilled among us" (v 1). Luke is talking about events that kept (or "fulfilled") previously-made promises. These events happened "among us" – that is, in (roughly) the time and place that this book was being written in. In other words, Luke is referring back to Old Testament prophecies – such as the one in Isaiah 9, written 700 years before – and saying that Jesus fulfilled them. The fact that these centuries-old prophecies in the Old Testament had come true shows us that the Bible, although written by human authors such as Luke, is inspired by God – the only one who is able to predict the future, because he controls the future. This helps us to have even greater confidence in what it tells us about Jesus.

Note: These questions may well not satisfy the more doubtful in your group when it comes to the historicity of the Bible. You don't need to worry about this at this point in the series. The aim here is to establish that Luke claimed to be writing history, not fables or allegories. At the end of the discussion, encourage guests to read "Can We Rely on Luke's Gospel?" on page 33 of their Handbook when they get home. For those who want to look into these things more, point them to a book such as *Is Jesus History?* by John Dickson, *Cold Case Christianity* by J. Warner Wallace, or *The Case for Christ* by Lee Strobel. It would be a good idea to have copies of one or more of these books to hand so that you can give them to guests.

So, the claim is that we're reading the words of a historian who had carefully researched the events of Jesus' life by speaking with eye witnesses – including the two events described in the film. Let's take another look at the second of those events.

Read Luke 8:40-42, 49-56

5. Trace the events of this passage. How might Jairus have felt at each of these points?

- **Verse 49:** Utter grief. His daughter is dead.

Synagogue | Where Jewish people gather for worship.

- **Verse 50:** Perhaps a mixture of hope and incredulity. He's told not to be afraid, and to believe that she can be healed – when she's dead!

- **Verses 51-53:** Perhaps hope based on trusting Jesus, or grief based on what everyone else thinks – or both.

- **Verse 54-55:** Can you imagine a happier moment for Jairus than when his deceased daughter stands up?!

- **Verse 56:** Luke tells us – astonishment.

6. What does this episode show us about:

- **Jesus' power?**

He can reverse death itself. Jesus came so that one day he can bring an end to sickness and death, and to all the pain, anxiety and grief that go along with them. He is the Mighty God come to earth.

- **Jesus' character?**

This is a harder question – but the aim is to see that Jesus chooses to use his power to help others, to bring life and to give hope; and that despite his great power, he wants to meet and speak with and help those who are struggling and desperate.

7. Earlier, we heard these events in Luke's Gospel described as "a thumbnail preview of an entirely new world" that Jesus will bring about one day. What hopeless situations do you see around you? What difference would it make to how we think and feel about those situations if Jesus were the Mighty God, who would one day step in to set everything right?

This question provides an opportunity to connect what we've seen in the Bible with peoples' lived experiences. In answer to the first part of the question, some people may feel comfortable sharing something very personal;

others may want to keep the conversation more general. Either is fine. The point is that – whether on a global scale or in our most private struggles – if we knew that one day Jesus would make things right in the way he made things right for Jairus, we could endure even the most seemingly hopeless situations in the present with hope. If you have time, this would be a great opportunity for you to share the difference that Jesus' promises for the future have made to you in otherwise hopeless situations.

8. **We've been thinking in this session about how the Bible claims that Jesus is the Mighty God, who gives us a hope worth having. What has particularly struck you as you've heard the films and looked at this part of Luke's Gospel?**

The aim of this question is to get a feel for where people are at in their response to what they've heard. If people want to talk more, encourage them to stick around at the end of the session.

Session 2 will be based on Luke 23. You could encourage group members to read more of Luke's Gospel before then – however much they want or are able to – and to come to the next session with any questions they may have.

SESSION 2
PEACE

- *Welcome the group to Session 2 of* Hope Explored. *If anyone missed the last session, briefly recap what happened and how this session will run, and make sure you've given everyone a copy of the Handbook and a Luke's Gospel or Bible.*

▷ **WATCH: Peace Part 1 (approx 5 mins)**

- We're all hoping for peace…
    - "out there"
    - "in here"
    - "between us"

- *Shalom* is the Bible's word for real peace – wholeness, harmony, completeness, prosperity, welfare, tranquillity, safety.

- But is lasting peace only a pipe dream?

💬 **DISCUSS**

This activity makes use of four picture prompts, each representing a place where people might look for peace. The pictures are provided in the Handbook, but to make this activity more dynamic, it's recommended that you print out or purchase a larger set of pictures (see page 12), so that they can be spread in front of you and passed between you as you discuss them together.

Ask the question below and then briefly explain the pictures and what they represent, but don't worry about nailing down specific definitions. Encourage guests to choose the one that resonates most with them. This is an opportunity to listen to guests as they share their understanding of peace, and the places they look in order to find it.

We've heard about some different ways in which we might be hoping for peace. But what about you? How do you think we can find peace?

Searching inside yourself: True peace can only come from inside ourselves; as we accept ourselves, let go of past regrets, and learn to be mindful in the present.

Getting away from it all: True peace can best be experienced when we switch off from all the stress and escape it all – whether by taking a trip, watching a movie, or shutting down our devices for a while.

Co-operating with others: True peace that will change our relationships will only come when we learn to work together with one another and engage in the give-and-take of compromise.

Campaigning for change: True peace that will transform the world for everyone can only be achieved when we stand up and demand that the system be changed.

It may be that members of your group find that a combination of these resonate, or they have their own ideas. To stimulate discussion, you could ask some follow-up questions: Where do you feel most at peace? What does peace mean to you? How would you answer differently if you were asked about the world in general or your life in particular? How would you answer the question from the end of the film we've just watched: "Is lasting peace only a pipe dream?"

**Searching inside
yourself**

**Getting away from
it all**

**Co-operating with
others**

**Campaigning for
change**

▷ **WATCH: Peace Part 2 (approx 21 mins)**

(Page 19 in the group members' Handbook.) Encourage people to make notes or write down questions as they watch the teaching film.

- We all want peace; but the problem is that we all want peace on our terms. We say, "My life, my rules".

- The problem is not just "horizontal". We lack peace on a "vertical" level, between ourselves and our Creator. Instead of saying, "Your world, your rules", we say, "My life, my rules". The Bible calls this sin.

- This matters because God is a God of justice, so God judges sin.

- But there is hope: a Prince of Peace – Jesus.

- Jesus was arrested, put on trial, and sentenced to execution by crucifixion. As he was dying, he told the criminal next to him, "Today you will be with me in paradise" (Luke 23:43). Jesus offered him a place of peace beyond death.

- How is this possible? Three steps to paradise: the criminal...
  1) acknowledges his wrongdoing,
  2) recognizes Jesus as the King, and
  3) cries out to Jesus for rescue.

- On the cross, Jesus absorbed God's anger at sin. This is how he can offer us peace.

- If we take Jesus up on his offer, we can start enjoying peace "in here", "between us" and, one day, "out there" too.

📖 EXPLORE

1. Where do you think our problem with peace comes from (if you think we have a problem at all)?

This question is intended to give guests space to respond to one of the key ideas in the teaching film: that humans are in a state of conflict with God, and our fraught horizontal relationships with one another are a symptom of our broken vertical relationship with him. Coming to recognize our own sinfulness is key to understanding the gospel, so this is an opportunity to get a feel for where guests are at on this.

Luke wants to show us that our problem is not just horizontal but vertical – and that as Jesus died, he was dealing with that lack of peace between us and God.

Read Luke 23:32-47

Luke records two supernatural events that happened while Jesus was on the cross. These were signs from God that pointed to what was happening vertically as Jesus died.

2. What was the first supernatural event, recorded in verses 44-45a? What does that suggest was happening vertically as Jesus died on the cross? (See note opposite for more information.)

It got dark, and (at least it looked like) the sun stopped shining for three hours, from noon till 3 p.m. The darkness showed that this was a time of God's judgment. As Jesus died on the cross, he was suffering not just the physical agony of crucifixion but the spiritual agony of being judged by his Father. God the Son was suffering the judgment of God the Father.

Casting lots | A way of making decisions randomly (similar to flipping a coin).

Messiah | A Greek word meaning "anointed one"; the King God had promised would rescue his people.

Centuries before, God had spoken to his people through one of his prophets, named Amos. God announced how people could know that his judgment on humanity's sin and on their conflict with him had come: "'In that day,' declares the Sovereign LORD, 'I will make the sun go down at noon and darken the earth in broad daylight'" (Amos 8:9).

God had also told his people to build a "temple" in Jerusalem – a building where he would dwell among them. But, as part of the temple, he had instructed them to put up a huge curtain at least 30 feet (9m) wide and 30 feet high. This curtain functioned as a "KEEP OUT" sign – the perfect God was present on one side of the curtain, and imperfect people could not pass through the curtain to be with him.

3. **Look at what happened to the curtain in the second half of verse 45. What does this second supernatural event suggest Jesus' death had achieved?**

The curtain of the temple tore in two. Because Jesus took the judgment for sin, the curtain tore to show that there is now nothing preventing humanity from coming into God's presence. There is now nothing keeping humans from being at peace with God because Jesus' death can deal with, bear, and remove their sin. You could remind your group of the image in the Part 1 film of *shalom* being like taking down the fence between neighbours. Jesus' death "took down the fence" between us and God.

4. **Jesus speaks three times in this passage. What does each tell us about him?**

   • **Verse 34**

Even at the moment of greatest rejection from all those around him, and in the greatest pain imaginable, Jesus is still hoping for and praying for people to be forgiven. This is a glimpse of the amazing love that he had (and has) for people – even people who hated him.

- **Verse 43**

Jesus is able to welcome people into paradise (a place of perfect peace beyond death) – even people who have spent their lives in conflict with God and others, like this criminal. Jesus is able to do this because paradise is his "kingdom".

- **Verse 46**

To the end, Jesus trusted God. Having borne the judgment for sin, he trusted God with his death. Notice that he does not fear death or fight it. To the end, Jesus was in control. It looks as though he chose the moment of his own death.

5. In what ways did the various people around the three crosses respond to Jesus?

- **"The people" (verse 35)**

The crowd stood watching. The death of Jesus seems to have left them unaffected – they were interested at best, but it made no great difference to them.

- **"The rulers" (verse 35)**

They sneered at Jesus. They felt assured that they were at peace with God and therefore had no need of Jesus. They saw the cross as a failure and Jesus as not worthy of their respect, let alone of their worship of him as God.

- **"The soldiers" (verses 36-37)**

They mocked Jesus. Despite being at the other end of the social spectrum from the rulers, they adopted a very similar attitude. They saw Jesus dying on the cross as proof that Jesus wasn't a king or anyone special – when, in fact, the opposite was true.

• "The centurion" (verse 47)

He praised God. This hard-bitten military officer, who had doubtless fought in several campaigns and seen many men die, realized that this death was different. He understood that Jesus was "righteous", meaning innocent. He seems to have realized that Jesus was innocent of the charge of making up his claim to be God's Son and God's King. Jesus was, in fact, guilty only of being who he said he was.

6. Which of those reactions best represents the way you're responding to Jesus at the moment?

This is an opportunity for guests to share where they think they stand in relation to Jesus.

7. On the night Jesus was arrested, his disciples had let him down, denied him and deserted him. Yet after Jesus had risen from death (which we'll be thinking about more in the next session), he greeted them with the words "Peace be with you" (Luke 24:36).

• **How did Jesus make peace possible by dying on the cross?**

Encourage your group to summarize how Jesus achieved peace between his people and God through dying on the cross.

Jesus, God the Son, died to bear the judgment of God the Father against the way in which all humanity has treated God and treated each other. In dying in the darkness, under divine judgment, Jesus took the punishment people deserve for sin. And in doing so, he is able to offer us peace with God, eternally. That is what the tearing of the temple curtain signified, and what his words to the criminal promised. So he was able to say to his followers, who had let him down, denied him, and deserted him, "Peace".

• **How do you think it felt for the disciples to hear that greeting? What would it take for you to receive that same peace from Jesus today?**

The disciples are conspicuous by their absence from the scene at the cross. Luke mentions the women specifically alongside unnamed followers but not the Twelve (Luke 23:49). Although we know that John at least was there (John 19:26), we're told that when Jesus was initially arrested, they all ran away (Mark 14:50), and Peter denied even knowing Jesus (Luke 22:54-62). So to hear Jesus' greeting of peace must have been a tremendous relief. We've seen that we too are undeserving of Jesus' peace offer. But Jesus does offer us peace. All we have to do in order to share in the disciples' relief, and the criminal's assurance, is to take the three "steps" outlined in the teaching film: acknowledge our wrongdoing, recognize Jesus as King, and cry out to him for rescue.

8. **We've been thinking in this session about how the Bible claims that Jesus is the Prince of Peace, who came to fulfil our hope of peace. What has particularly struck you as you've watched the films and looked at this part of Luke's Gospel?**

SESSION 3
PURPOSE

- *Welcome the group to Session 3 of* Hope Explored. *If anyone missed the last session, briefly recap what happened.*

▷ **WATCH: Purpose Part 1 (approx 6 mins)**

- We all want our lives to mean something. We all need purpose. But the reality of death makes us wonder, "What's the point?"

- In our 21st-century Western culture, we tend to deal with the problem of death in one of three ways:
    - We deny it.
    - We downplay it.
    - We despair about it.

- To find meaning in life, we need an answer to death.

🗨 **DISCUSS**

During this activity we will be discussing four pictures, each representing a place where people might look for purpose. The pictures are provided in the Handbook, but to make this activity more dynamic, it's recommended that you print out or purchase a larger set of pictures (see page 12), so that they can be spread in front of you and passed round as you discuss them together.

Ask the question below, and then briefly explain the pictures and what they represent, but don't worry about nailing down specific definitions. Encourage guests to choose the one which resonates most with them. This is an opportunity to listen to guests as they share their understanding of purpose and where they find a sense of meaning.

We've heard about some different attitudes towards purpose in life. But what about you? Where do you look for a sense of purpose?

Building a successful career: A sense of purpose comes from being successful and having a comfortable lifestyle.

Pursuing happiness: The purpose of life is to enjoy ourselves, have fun, embrace different experiences and pursue happiness.

Raising a family: A sense of purpose comes from caring for and nurturing loved ones.

Leaving a legacy: Purpose in life comes from making the world a better place for those around us and the generations that will follow.

It may be that members of your group find that a combination of these resonate, or they have their own ideas. To stimulate discussion, you could ask some follow-up questions: Have any significant life events changed your sense of purpose (e.g. having children)? How does your view of purpose differ from that of your friends or people in general?

Building a successful career

Pursuing happiness

Raising a family

Leaving a legacy

▷ WATCH: Purpose Part 2 (approx 18 mins)

(Page 27 in the group members' Handbook.) Encourage people to make notes or write down questions as they watch the teaching film.

- Jesus died on Friday. On Sunday morning, something happened that can rob death of its power and give life the purpose we long for.

- When the women arrived at Jesus' tomb, it was empty. Two angels told them, "He is not here, he has risen" (Luke 24:6).

- This is hard to believe – then as now. The disciples dismissed it as "non-sense", but in the years that followed they gave their lives for this claim. So what changed?

- Later on Sunday evening, Jesus appeared to his disciples and proved that it was really him, really risen.

- Is there a better explanation for the empty tomb and for the transformation in Jesus' followers? The Bible doesn't ask you to shut your eyes and make a leap of faith. Instead, it encourages you to open your eyes, look at the evidence, and make a step of faith.

- If the resurrection is true, then it is wonderful. It means that Jesus can be our "Everlasting Father", who sorts out death and gives us meaningful work with an eternal impact. "Always give yourselves fully to the work of the Lord, because you know that your labour in the Lord is not in vain" (1 Corinthians 15:58).

- Will you take Jesus to be your "Wonderful Counsellor"?

APPENDICES

QUESTIONS ABOUT
CHRISTIAN BELIEF

How do you know that God exists?

- Many philosophical and scientific arguments have been used over the years to show that believing in God is rational and sensible. But ultimately, even the best of these lead only to general belief in a God, not specifically to the God of the Bible. It is usually more helpful to talk about Jesus and his claim to be God.

- We can know God exists because he became a man: Jesus Christ. This is the core of Jesus' answer to Philip's question in John 14:8-9. It's worth looking this up and reading it together if the question arises.

- Jesus was a real person who lived in Palestine 2,000 years ago – the historical evidence for this stacks up (see next question).

- Jesus claimed to be God (e.g. John 5:18; 20:28-29), and his actions bore out that claim. Check out his claims as you read Luke and come to *Hope Explored*.

Why should we believe what the Bible says?

- Try not to get involved in defending passages from all over the Bible. Instead, start with the reliability of the Gospels. See "Can We Rely on Luke's Gospel?" on page 71 of this Leader's Handbook. If we can rely on the Gospels, and what Jesus says in the Gospels about the trustworthiness of Scripture, then it makes sense to trust the Bible as a whole.

- Historical evidence in the New Testament is confirmed at a number of points by non-Christian historical writers – e.g. Tacitus and Josephus – and also by archaeological evidence.

- The New Testament documents were written soon after the events they describe.

- This New Testament documentation is extensive, coming from as many as ten authors, eight of whom wrote independently of each other.

- The documents are historical in character as well as theological. They contain many verifiable details of the time and culture in which they were written.

- Textual criticism shows that the text of these documents has come down to us intact from the era in which they were written.

- The writers were people who suffered

and died for what they believed, and were also of very high moral standing. They believed in telling the truth. It is highly unlikely they would make up these stories or even "imagine" them.

- The Gospels are very uncomplimentary about the disciples who assisted in writing them. For example, Peter helped Mark write his Gospel – and yet Peter is shown to be a coward (Mark 14:66-72). Given that Peter was a leader in the early church, why would he include something like this? Unless, of course, it was just the inconvenient truth.

- The Gospel accounts are too detailed to be legends. They're packed full of tiny details that apparently serve no purpose, unless explained simply as eye-witness details. Modern novels sometimes have this level of detail, but they didn't exist until about 300 years ago; it's unprecedented in an ancient document. The author C. S. Lewis (once Professor of English Literature at both Oxford and Cambridge) said, "I have been reading poems, romances, vision literature, legends and myths all my life. I know what they are like. I know none of them are like this."

Don't all good people go to heaven?

- What is "good"? How good is "good enough"?
- Some of us are better than others, but no one meets God's standards (see Romans 3:23).

- We are not good because our hearts are "sin factories" (Mark 7:21-22).
- People who think they're "good enough" for heaven don't realize that they've broken what Jesus calls the first and most important of all God's commands: "Love the Lord your God with all your heart and with all your soul and with all your mind and with all your strength" (Mark 12:28-30). Rather than loving God, we love other things more (see the story of the rich man meeting Jesus in Mark 10:17-22). We may be "good" relative to others, but we can't be good enough for heaven if we break God's most important command.
- The opposite is, in fact, true. "Good" people go to hell; bad people go to heaven. Those who think they are good, and rely on that, will be lost. Only those who know they are lost are able to receive forgiveness and eternal life from Christ.

Why would a good God send people to hell?

- God is utterly holy and good. His character is what decides right and wrong in the universe.
- God must judge everyone. He would not be a just God if he ignored wrongdoing or evil. He will judge fairly and well.
- We know that punishments ought to fit the crime. Someone who murders deserves a worse punishment than someone who runs a red light. Is it possible that the reason we think hell is unfair is

because we don't realize how serious our sin is?

- Jesus is the most loving person who ever lived, but it is he who teaches most about the reality of hell. He does so because he knows it is real and doesn't want us to suffer the inevitable consequences of our rebellion against God.

- God has judged his Son, Jesus, on the cross. As a result, he went through hell, so we don't have to. When he died on the cross, he was dying in our place. For those who turn to him, Jesus took the punishment we deserve, so we can know God and enjoy him forever.

- If we understood how holy God is, we would be asking the opposite question: how can God allow anyone into heaven?

If God forgives everything, does that mean I can do what I like?

- God offers us forgiveness so that we can know and enjoy him. Why would we want to "do what we like" if, by doing so, it keeps us from enjoying him to the full and puts us in danger of judgment?

How can we be sure that there is life after death?

- The Bible teaches that everyone will be resurrected after death in order to face judgment (Hebrews 9:27). For those who know and love Christ, there is nothing to fear, because the one appointed as Judge (Acts 17:31) is also the one who gave his life for them.

- Who do you trust for accurate information about life beyond the grave? The person who has been there and come back. If Jesus has been raised from the dead, then those who trust in him will also be delivered from death. (See John 11:25.)

What about other religions?

- Sincerity is not truth. People can be sincerely wrong.

- If the different religions contradict each other (which they do at several major points), they cannot all be right.

- The question really is: has God revealed himself, and if so, how? Jesus claimed to be the unique revelation of God. He claimed to be God in the flesh. Are his claims valid? If Jesus is God, then, logically, other religions must be wrong.

- Jesus claims he is the only way (John 14:6).

- Religions can do many good things: provide comfort, help, social bonding, etc. But all of them – apart from Christianity – teach that we must DO something in order to "earn" our place in heaven.

- By contrast, Jesus claims that we can never "earn" our way to heaven by doing good things. He claims that the only way we can know and enjoy God forever is if we trust in what HE (Jesus) has done on our behalf, not in what WE have done.

What about those who have never heard about Jesus?

- We can trust God to be just; he will judge people according to their response to what they know.
- Everyone has received some revelation, even if only from the created world (see Romans 1:18-19).
- Those who have had more revealed to them will be held more responsible (Matthew 11:20-24).
- You have heard, so you must do something about it – and leave the others to God, who will treat them fairly.

Isn't faith just a psychological crutch?

- It is true that faith in Christ provides an enormous psychological crutch! It gives hope, meaning and joy, even in the face of suffering and death. It is one of life's greatest joys to know for certain that you are perfectly known and yet perfectly loved by the Creator of the universe.
- But that doesn't mean Christian faith is "wishful thinking" – some sort of imaginary story created to make us feel better in the face of life's hardships.
- On the contrary, Christian faith is founded on historical events: the life, death and resurrection of Jesus. The truth of these events – and therefore the truth of Christianity – doesn't depend on whether or not we "need" them to be true.

Why does God allow suffering?

- Much suffering is a direct result of our own sinfulness (e.g. that caused by drunkenness, greed, lust, etc.).
- But some is not (see John 9:1-3).
- All suffering results from the fallen nature of our world (see Romans 8:18-25).
- God uses suffering to discipline and strengthen his children (see Hebrews 12:7-11; Romans 5:3-5).
- God also uses suffering to wake people up so that they understand that there is a judgment coming to our pain-filled world (Luke 13:1-5).
- Unlike many other "gods", the God of the Bible knows intimately what it is like to suffer. God the Son suffered loneliness, grief, temptation, alienation from loved ones, mockery, isolation, bereavement, hunger, thirst, homelessness, mental anguish and the worst physical agonies humans have been able to invent. As a result, he relates to and sympathizes with our deepest pain (Hebrews 4:15). He is not distant from it, or disinterested in it.
- But the God of the Bible does more than show mere sympathy; he has done something decisive to end all human suffering. Jesus suffered and died so that those who know and love him can one day enjoy a new creation, where there will be no suffering or pain of any kind.
- Though we don't know all the reasons why God allows suffering in every case, it seems reasonable to assume that our "not knowing" doesn't necessarily mean suffering must be pointless. At the time Jesus suffered and died, the disciples

FILM SCRIPTS

Session 1 | Hope | Part 1

It's the feeling you get as a kid in the last week of school before the summer – or as an adult, when you've only got two days left at work before a holiday. Or how it feels a couple of minutes before the final whistle, when you know your team's going to win. Even though the game's not over, your excitement builds with every pass and tackle as the clock counts down to certain victory.

That's hope. And there are few emotions more powerful. Hope is a spark inside you that brings a smile to your lips, a light that shows on your face, a feeling that lifts your head and pulls you forward.

Maybe you can remember a time when you knew that something good was on its way: that some happy thing was going to happen to you or the people you love.

That, right there, is hope.

And it's a strange emotion, because in that moment nothing has changed and yet everything has changed. That thing on the horizon of your future lifts your mood in the present. So, while circumstances remain the same for now, you go about your day like you're walking on air.

Real hope is not a vague optimism but a joyful confidence – an expectation for the future that is worth working for, worth waiting for. Hope's a wonderful thing, a powerful thing. It's what keeps us alive. History's greatest survival stories show that when we have something to live for we can persevere through even the hardest of circumstances.

That's why there are few things that crush us more than when our hopes are dashed. That sinking feeling in your stomach when the application gets rejected or the sale falls through or the test results come back, and all your happy daydreams dissolve in a moment. I'll never forget the phone call my dad got when I was sixteen years old that broke the news of a family tragedy. My uncle had been killed in an accident. It hit me like a ton of bricks.

Dashed hopes are hard to bear. And so are disappointed hopes. Perhaps you know how it feels when you do get what you've been dreaming of, only to find it's not all you thought it would be. You finally get the job, or the relationship, or the retirement that you'd been hoping for and… it just doesn't deliver the satisfaction it promised. So you set your sights on something else, and the whole cycle starts over again. Hope drives us – until it disappoints us.

And perhaps you've even met someone with no hope at all. Someone who's been knocked down too low for too long, and now there's no good thing on the horizon – nothing to lift their head. Hopelessness is awful. Maybe that's been you – in the past, or perhaps even right now.

We all need hope. It's what keeps us alive. So we need to find a hope worth having, that won't get dashed and that won't disappoint us. What does that kind of hope look like?

A hope worth having is one that is true. We need to be confident that it really will happen. Not a fantasy but reality; not maybe but sure.

A hope worth having is one that delivers what it promises. When we get there, it needs to meet our expectations and be worth all the effort. The thing we're hoping for should be every bit as good as we'd imagined it would be.

And a hope worth having has to be for something that will last. Otherwise the joy will fade, and we'll have to start hoping for something else.

Hope like that proves elusive to many of us. Yet lots of people say they've found it. In all humility, I would, too. That's why these three sessions are called *Hope Explored*. Because a hope worth having is what the Christian faith claims to offer. It's an invitation to put your hope in a future that is better than anything else you could imagine.

Christianity is not about a feeling in my tummy or a blind faith in defiance of all the data. Christian hope is a joyful expectation for the future, based on true events in the past, which changes everything about my present. That's what real hope is: a hope worth having.

And if you're not convinced of that, welcome. Whatever you do or don't believe, we're so glad you're here. This series is for you. This is your opportunity to explore, to discuss, to question, to discover. This is *Hope Explored*.

Session 1 | Hope | Part 2

Where do you think the world is going? Sometimes it looks like things are getting better, other times things seem to be getting worse – and a lot of the time, it looks like chaos!

But what if I were to ask you a more personal version of that question: Where do you think your life is going?

Our answer to both of those questions will partly depend on our experience of life so far. As we look at the world around us, it's easy to spot the many good things we humans enjoy. I call them the Fs: fun, food, family, fitness, friendship, falling in love.

But even if you've lived the most sheltered life, you'll have encountered some of the Ds as well: disappointment, death, divorce, depression, disease, disorder in the world. In a word: darkness.

The Bible is 100% realistic about the darkness we experience. But it also speaks of hope. Listen to these words from a part of the Bible called the book of Isaiah, chapter 9 verse 2:

"The people walking in darkness have seen a great light; on those living in the land of deep darkness a light has dawned."

Every dark path needs a light at the end of the tunnel. Every sad story needs a turning point if it's going to have a happy ending. Every person needs a hope worth having.

And that's exactly the kind of hope this verse is talking about. It was written in around 700 BC, to an oppressed people living in Judah, in modern-day Israel, just east of the Mediterranean Sea. It's part of what's called a prophecy: a message from God to his people, delivered via a human messenger called Isaiah.

Isaiah's message was that someone was coming who could turn things around for hopeless people; someone was coming who could bring light into the darkness. Listen to this:

"He will be called Wonderful Counsellor, Mighty God, Everlasting Father, Prince of Peace."

Now, I don't know whether you believe that there's a God out there. Many of us like to think that there is. Or, at the very least, we hope that there's something more than our material universe: some bigger reality that makes sense of the story of life on earth. But if there is a God out there, it would be great if he proved it.

And the claim of the Bible is: he has. The Bible says that 2,000 years ago someone showed up who was that person God had promised through Isaiah to send – the Wonderful Counsellor, Mighty God, Everlasting Father, Prince of Peace, came to earth. And that turning point in history can give us hope today.

I don't expect you to believe that just because I say it. In fact, please don't believe it just because I say it. Instead, I'd love you to look with me at some of the evidence for that claim: a Gospel, a historical biography of a man named Jesus, who was born in Israel, grew up in an obscure town, and started his working life as a carpenter, but went on to become the figure at the centre of the world's largest religion. The book is called Luke – named after the doctor who wrote it. He interviewed eye witnesses of what this Jesus said and did, and wrote it up, in around AD 60.

In Luke chapter 8 he tells us about one single day in Jesus' life. We're going to look briefly at just two snapshots from that day and see how they relate to one of the titles Isaiah used: Mighty God.

The first incident takes place on a lake. Luke 8 verse 22:

"One day Jesus said to his disciples, 'Let us go over to the other side of the lake.' So they got into a boat and set out. As they sailed, he fell asleep. A squall came down on the lake, so that the boat was being swamped, and they were in great danger.

"The disciples went and woke him, saying, 'Master, Master, we're going to drown!'

"He got up and rebuked the wind and the raging waters; the storm subsided, and all was calm. 'Where is your faith?' he asked his disciples.

"In fear and amazement they asked one another, 'Who is this? He commands even the winds and the water, and they obey him.'"

Imagine the disciples' desperation as their routine boat trip turns into a life-threatening emergency. This is not just your average storm.

In fact it's more like a hurricane – it's what happens when the cold air from the mountains meets the warm air around the sea of Galilee. It produces this type of typhoon on the surface of the water. But when faced with the horrors of this hurricane, Jesus stands up and says, *Quiet, be still.* And it is.

Here is a man with the power to control the uncontrollable – here is a man who can turn things around. The wind and the waves don't have ears, and yet when Jesus speaks, he can calm them.

So the disciples are left asking the right question: "Who is this?" Who can do something like that? What category do you put him in? If he can calm a storm with a word, he's clearly not simply a teacher, or a philosopher, or a healer. Who is he?

This matters to us, because it's not just about lakes and storms and fishing boats. It's about the things that make you lie awake at night because they're out of your control. The question marks that cloud your future. The hard things that threaten to overwhelm you.

Wouldn't it be amazing news if there were a Mighty God with the power to control them? That wouldn't make hard things easy. But it would be reassuring that behind the universe stands a Mighty God who is running the show, who is working things out.

So consider this: could this man Jesus be that Mighty God? Could it be that Jesus is the Mighty God, promised by Isaiah, now walking on the earth he created and commanding it with his words?

Maybe, though, the calming of the storm was a stroke of luck. A happy coincidence. A one-off. Let's look at a second snapshot from later that day, after Jesus had got off the boat and walked into a town. Luke 8 verse 41:

"A man named Jairus, a synagogue leader, came and fell at Jesus' feet, pleading with him to come to his house because his only daughter, a girl of about twelve, was dying."

There's nothing more agonising than a parent losing a child. This little girl – she's Jairus' pride and joy, the light of the house. But now she's seriously sick. And there's nothing Jairus can do. He'd fix this if he could, but he can't. He's desperate.

So he throws himself at the feet of this man he'd heard has miracle powers, and begs for help.

Now, if Jesus is just a carpenter, what can he do? He can offer to make a lovely coffin. But the question is, can he do more than that?

Jairus is about to find out. They set out for his house together, but Jesus gets delayed on the way, and before they get there, Jairus hears those horrific words that every parent dreads.

"Someone came from the house of Jairus, the synagogue leader. 'Your daughter is dead,' he said. 'Don't bother the teacher anymore.'"

It's like a punch in the stomach. All Jairus' worst nightmares have come true. His wife will never be the same again.

But then Jesus speaks:

"Don't be afraid; just believe, and she will be healed."

When someone's lost a child, you don't play games with the parents. This is a big claim. He'd better be able to deliver. He'd better be more than a carpenter. What's he going to do?

"When he arrived at the house of Jairus, he did not let anyone go in with him except Peter, John and James, and the child's father and mother. Meanwhile, all the people were wailing and mourning for

are under the same sentence? We are punished justly, for we are getting what our deeds deserve. But this man has done nothing wrong.'

"Then he said, 'Jesus, remember me when you come into your kingdom.' Jesus answered him, 'Truly I tell you, today you will be with me in paradise.'"

"Today you will be with me in paradise." When you think about it, that's an outrageous offer. This criminal is under the sentence of death. He's likely a murderer, a thief and a terrorist. He's been cast out of society and nailed up on a cross to slowly suffocate to death.

Yet what does Jesus promise him? A place of peace. That's what the word "paradise" is getting at. It's harmony, wholeness and tranquillity.

So how can one dying man look across at another dying man and make such a promise? How can we find peace?

Well, in the verses leading up to that peace offer, there are three steps – think of them as three steps to paradise, if you like.

We see the first one in verses 41 and 42. The criminal says, "Don't you fear God? … We are punished justly, for we are getting what our deeds deserve."

So he doesn't say, *Look, I'm a victim*. He doesn't say, *I'm innocent*. It's as if his journal has been opened and his heart has been exposed. There's a problem in his world, and that problem is him. He says, *I deserve to be here. I'm being punished justly, not only by the arm of the state, but by the arm of God*. He acknowledges his wrongdoing. That's the first step.

You don't meet many people this honest

about their own flaws. I don't know what you made of all that talk of sin and judgment earlier. But the thing is, Christianity will never make sense until you get to the point where you look at your wrongdoing and say, "Actually, I've been living with a 'My life, my rules' attitude, and I deserve judgment."

Our culture finds this unpalatable. We live in a world that laughs at sin – just as the other criminal mocked Jesus back then. But that doesn't change the truth: that our conflict with God is real, is serious, and it's our fault. And admitting this can actually be wonderfully freeing, as we'll see next. So that's step one – we acknowledge our wrongdoing.

Second, the criminal recognizes Jesus as the king – the Mighty God, come to earth. He sees in verse 41 that "this man has done nothing wrong." And then in verse 42 he says, "Jesus, remember me when you come into your kingdom". When this criminal looks at Jesus, he doesn't see a desperate man at the end of his life but a king with a royal pardon to bestow. A King who can calm a storm, who can raise the dead, and who will rule over a paradise beyond death. I wonder what you see as you look at Jesus?

And in the third step, this dying man cries out to Jesus for rescue. He says, "Jesus, remember me when you come into your kingdom."

It's not that he just wants Jesus to think of him – he wants Jesus to act for him.

Think of a married couple. If one of them says, "Remember, darling, it's our anniversary next week", they're not expecting their partner merely to remember that fact but to do something about it – to book the table or buy the flowers.

This criminal sees that Jesus is a King with a kingdom beyond death – an eternal place of total peace. And when Jesus gets there, the man wants Jesus to act for him. He asks Jesus to welcome him, a condemned criminal, into that kingdom. This criminal offers nothing, but he asks for everything.

And what does Jesus say in response? He doesn't say, *Sorry – I'm just a man like you. I can't help you.*

He doesn't say, *Well, I'll tell you how you can save yourself. Live a decent life. Say your prayers, love your neighbour, go to church, and then you'll book your place in heaven.*

He doesn't say, *You decided to reject me and my rule in your life. You made your bed, and now you'll lie in it.*

No – Jesus says, "Truly, I tell you today you will be with me in paradise". No conditions. No qualifications. No delays. Just total acceptance, total forgiveness, total peace with God. The criminal offers nothing, but he receives everything.

Yet this forgiveness isn't free. Yes, it's free for the criminal, but it costs Jesus his life. Look at what happens next in verse 44.

"It was now about noon, and darkness came over the whole land until three in the afternoon, for the sun stopped shining … Jesus called out with a loud voice, 'Father, into your hands I commit my spirit.' When he had said this, he breathed his last."

Three hours of total darkness – it's not an eclipse but a supernatural sign of God's judgment against sin. But this judgment isn't falling on the people who deserve it. Instead, what's happening is that God is handing Jesus over to the consequences of other peoples' sin – of my sin. Jesus is paying for all the wrong in my journal.

In a world of conflict and rebellion, Jesus was the only person always to have kept the peace. If Jesus had kept a journal, you wouldn't find any wrongdoing in it. But on the cross, he experienced God's judgment – as if he had my sinful record. Jesus willingly paid the price so that he can offer peace.

Here's a picture of how this works. A few years ago, as I was cycling in London, my front wheel jammed between the bars of a road drain. The bike stopped dead, I flew over the handlebars, and I hit the surface of the road head first. A doctor I saw afterwards said that if I had not been wearing a helmet, I'd probably have been killed. But I was wearing a helmet. It got smashed to pieces, but I just stood up and I was fine. Because of the bicycle helmet, I was alive.

Bicycle helmets are designed to absorb the energy of an impact so that it's not transmitted to your head. But in order to absorb that impact, the helmet has to shatter. So when I crashed, my helmet was destroyed by the impact that would have killed me. And that is a small and inadequate picture of what Jesus did on the cross. Here was God, taking his own judgment, bearing his own anger, taking into himself the darkness that should be mine.

The Prince of Peace experienced the darkness as he died so that the criminal next to him would not have to endure it after he died. Instead, that criminal could enter into God's place of peace for eternity.

Peace with God is what Jesus offered the criminal – and peace with God is what he continues to offer today. The steps to peace haven't changed. If we acknowledge our wrongdoing, accept Jesus as

King, and ask him to rescue us, we too can know peace. That's all we have to do, but we do have to do it.

And if we take Jesus up on this offer, then everything changes.

It starts "in here". It means you can face the world with joy and confidence – because you're at peace with the one who owns the place! When you mess up, you don't need to try to ignore it, or seek to hide it, or work to excuse it. You can be honest. This is wonderfully freeing.

And that changes things "between us". God's Spirit gets to work in the lives of his people, making friends out of enemies, repairing broken relationships. It means we can learn to forgive others because we know how much we have been forgiven by God. It means we're able to say those two phrases that are so crucial to relational harmony: "I'm sorry, I was wrong" and "That's ok, I forgive you." That won't always be easy, and it won't always look perfect, and it will often take time, but God's peace does give us real hope for all our relationships.

And one day, there'll be peace "out there". There's hope for our bitter and broken world. History is heading somewhere, and heading somewhere good. The Bible says that there will be a day when the Prince of Peace will restore the whole creation to a state of *shalom* – of real peace – fully and finally and forever.

Peace "in here," secure before God. Peace "between us," as we live in his world. Peace "out there" one day in a restored creation. And all because of peace with God, won for us by Jesus, the Prince of Peace. His death means that as we look at the journal of our lives and see the evidence of our sin, we can say to him with confidence, "I'm sorry, I was wrong." And

in return, we can hear with comfort, "That's ok, I forgive you".

That's the hope of peace that Jesus invites us to know for ourselves, just as he offered it to the rebel on the cross: "Truly I tell you, today you will be with me in paradise."

Session 3 | Purpose | Part 1

I was at a school reunion not long ago, reflecting on the past 35 years. (I know it's hard to believe by looking at my hair that I left school 35 years ago, but it's true!)

The friend I was talking with was brutally honest about his life as he rewound it in his mind. He said, "I've spent my life just going from one thing to another. I've just lived." And it felt to him like it had been a bit empty – like it had all been an anticlimax.

I remember feeling something similar when I was clearing out my parents' house after they'd died. I'll never forget the experience. In one sense, it was darkly comic. My friend who was helping me dropped a piece of furniture on his foot and broke a toe, and we crashed the removal van halfway through the job and had to pay for the damage.

But the experience has stayed with me for deeper reasons too. I remember the two sofas which for so long had been the centre of my mum and dad's living room, the centre of their home – and I had to watch them go toppling into the skip. Then there were the gifts that my father had been given on his retirement – tokens of a long and respected career – and I had no idea what to do with them. There were drawers full of photos of a growing family and happy holidays – and I knew those moments would never be recaptured.

In one sense, the house was full of signs

of two lives well lived. But as I surveyed these objects that my parents had so cherished in their lifetime, I couldn't help thinking, "What was the point of that?" All the trophies won, all the milestones marked, all the Christmases celebrated – what did it matter? The reality of death suddenly made the preceding eight decades of life seem strangely meaningless. My parents were here, and then they weren't. It would be the same for me and for my broken-toed friend. What was it all for?

All of us hope that our lives mean something. We want to make a difference. Leave a legacy. Build something worthwhile. We need purpose. That's what gets us out of bed in the morning and what gets us through the tough times.

But there's a huge problem that gets in the way of our search for the meaning of life. It's the reality that life ends. It sounds depressing, but it's true. As cleaning out my parents' house showed me, death mocks everything we achieve and accomplish and accumulate.

And that's why every culture in history has had to find a way to deal with the reality of death. Here's how 21st-century Western societies do it.

First, we deny it. We just pretend it's not there. Near where I live, there's a great playground. It's where I take the kids sometimes on a Sunday afternoon. For centuries it was a cemetery, right in the middle of the community. But now that's been paved over. They've moved the cemetery miles away, behind a high wall, away from sight, and they've put a playground in instead. It's symbolic of what we do with death as a culture. We hide it. We pretend it won't happen.

Then we try to downplay it. Think of all the ways we describe death to make it sound less final – less of a full stop. As Professor Dumbledore remarks in one of JK Rowling's Harry Potter books, "To the well-organized mind, death is but the next great adventure."

But then, reality intrudes. We go to a colleague's funeral. A loved one dies. We ourselves get a terminal diagnosis. We can't deny death's reality any longer or downplay how much it hurts. Death is not an adventure for those left behind – it's agony, isn't it? Death robs us of our loved ones – and people who love us are so hard to come by.

When we confront that reality, all that's left is to start to despair about death – because death drains life of meaning. In the haunting words of playwright William Shakespeare:

Life's but a walking shadow, a poor player,
That struts and frets his hour upon the stage,
And then is heard no more. It is a tale
Told by an idiot, full of sound and fury,
Signifying nothing.

None of us want our lives to signify nothing. We want them to mean something. But if we want to find meaning in life, we need a reason to hope that something comes next – we need an answer to death.

As a pastor in central London I spend time with a lot of grieving people. During the COVID-19 pandemic, a neighbour of mine died, and so I went with the widow to register the death. The woman across the counter doing the paperwork was so sympathetic. She said, "It's so sad to hear about your husband. I lost my dad last year. I hope he's in a better place, but no one has come back from the dead to prove it."

and feet; he invites them to touch him to check; and then he eats something. And he tells them that what he's doing was predicted hundreds of years before by prophets like Isaiah. And that's just this one occasion! Jesus was seen and spoken to on numerous occasions, sometimes by small groups, and at least once by a gathering of hundreds.

That's why the first followers of Jesus were willing to die for the claim that Jesus was alive. They weren't just dying for something they believed to be true, like martyrs of whatever religion or cause today, but because of something they'd seen to be true. There's a big difference.

I hope you're beginning to see that the evidence that Jesus really did rise from the dead actually stacks up. And this matters, because Christian hope is based on true events in the past. So we need to be convinced this really did happen.

And if you're not, well, here's another way to think about it. Ask yourself: is there a better historical explanation for the incontestable events of the first Easter Sunday?

First, the empty tomb. No one, including Jesus' enemies, denied at the time that Jesus' body was gone. So if Jesus did not rise again, where did his body go?

Likewise, to deny the resurrection we're also going to have to find a different explanation for the transformation in Jesus' followers and the explosive growth of Christianity in the 1st century. What else could have caused that?

So to believe in the resurrection is not to follow a preconception or prejudice – it is to follow the historical evidence. The Bible doesn't ask you to shut your eyes and make a leap of faith. Instead, it encourages you to open your eyes, look at the evidence, and make a step of faith.

Because if this is true, then it's wonderful. It changes everything.

If Jesus rose from the dead, he really is the Mighty God and the Prince of Peace who Isaiah promised. And he offers to be our "Everlasting Father" too – that's the third of the four titles Isaiah gives him.

I don't know what kind of dad you had. Maybe you had a great dad. Maybe yours just wasn't there, or if he was, you wished that he wasn't. But the image of a father in the Bible is of someone who sorts things out. They care for you and about you. They get things done. They make sure the family's protected. That's what a good dad should do. He sorts things out. That's what the title "Everlasting Father" tells us about Jesus. He sorts out eternity. He sorts out the problem of death.

Because if Jesus got through death himself, he can get me through. In his resurrection, Jesus is like a needle that goes through a tapestry – he bursts through death and comes through the other side. And we're like the thread. If we're attached to him, we follow through. Yes, we'll still die. But like Jesus we'll burst through into glorious new life on the other side.

But it's not just that. As our Everlasting Father, Jesus invites us to be part of the family business. He says, *I'm going to give you work with an eternal impact.*

Not long after I became a Christian as a teenager, a friend showed me a verse from the Bible that totally changed my perspective on life. It was a real turning point. It's from part of the Bible where Paul, the writer, has just finished explaining about the evidence for the resurrection and how this guarantees that Christians will also live beyond death. Then he finishes by explaining how that hope for the future transforms what we do in the present: "Therefore, my dear brothers and sisters, stand firm. Let nothing move you. Always give yourselves fully to the work of the Lord, because you know that your labour in the Lord is not in vain."

Reading that verse for the first time was a real light-bulb moment for me. Jesus' resurrection gave me hope in the face of death. And that meant the idea of death no longer sapped life of all meaning. Nothing was in vain. Everything I did could be part of something that would last beyond my lifetime. I had a purpose to live for because I had a person to live for: Jesus Christ: the Mighty God, Everlasting Father, Prince of Peace.

Fast-forward 35 years to that conversation at my school reunion. My friend was right. My life has had real purpose. Jesus' resurrection means everything I do has meaning. Not because of what I do but because of who I do it for.

And Jesus extends that same invitation to you – to spend your life building something that lasts forever. If we find our significance in anything else, it will eventually let us down – but this won't. The resurrection is the great answer, the only answer, to our despair at death. And it means that we don't have to downplay or deny death, because Jesus has defeated death.

Our lives can be more than a few short sentences in the great sweep of history, scrunched up and forgotten once we're gone, discarded as meaningless. No, they can have real purpose. Because, when we live with Jesus as our Everlasting Father, all that we do with him and for him is woven into his bigger story – a story that only gets better beyond death.

So here's my question as I finish: will you ask Jesus to be for you the fourth description Isaiah gave him: your "Wonderful Counsellor"?

By "Counsellor", Isaiah means someone who takes direction of your life – the one you view as the authoritative expert, the person who calls the shots. All of us take someone as our counsellor: it may be a parent, a partner, a guru, a celebrity – most often, it's simply ourselves. But there's no counsellor as wonderful as Jesus.

Jesus gives hope – because he's the Mighty God, with the power to meet our deepest needs.

Jesus offers peace – because he's the Prince of Peace, who tears down the barrier between us and God.

And Jesus brings purpose – because he's the Everlasting Father, whose defeat of death gives life the meaning we long for.

So you can trust him to be your Wonderful Counsellor – to be the one who knows what's best and who shows you what's best, as you seek to live life his way. And if you're not sure of that yet, then please – keep exploring. Find out more about Jesus.

All of us are looking for a hope worth having. That's why we called this series *Hope Explored*. For Christians, Jesus' promise of life beyond death is what gives us real hope – it's what lights the spark inside us and lifts our head and pulls us forward towards the future.

And you too can live with a joyful expectation for the future, based on true events in the past, which changes everything about your present. Jesus invites you to be part of the great story of what he has done, is doing and will do.

That's not just hope explored. That's hope fulfilled.

ACKNOWLEDGEMENTS

Hope Explored Handbooks

Authors Alastair Gledhill, Rachel Jones, Carl Laferton and Rico Tice, with additional material by Barry Cooper

Designer André Parker

Hope Explored Films

Director Sam Kwan
Producer Janine Cobain
Presenter Rico Tice
Script development Rachel Jones
Screenplay Sam Kwan and Alastair Gledhill

Special Thanks

To the churches and individuals who trialled this material and gave such helpful feedback.

REGISTER YOUR COURSE AT
WWW.HOPE.EXPLO.RED

Visit the *Hope Explored* website to register your course and gain access to additional materials:

- **Digital picture prompts** for the discussion activity

- Outlines and **transcripts** of the teaching films

- A **sample presentation** for use when running *Hope Explored* online

- Guidance for **setting up your course**, including setting up a venue, inviting guests, and choosing and training leaders

- **Promotional materials** including trailers, logos and posters

Christianity Explored Ministries (CEM) aims to provide Christian churches and organizations worldwide with resources which explain the Christian faith clearly and relevantly from the Bible. CEM receives royalties from the sale of these resources, but is reliant on donations for the majority of its income. CEM is registered for charitable purposes in both the United Kingdom and the USA. **www.ceministries.org**

MORE COURSES AVAILABLE FROM

CHRISTIANITY
EXPLORED
MINISTRIES

Leader's kits contain everything you need
to evaluate the course.

For more information visit

www.ceministries.org

www.hope.explo.red